Teen
FAQ
Drugs

Teen FAQ Drugs

Ann Kramer

ARCTURUS

This edition first published in 2010 by Arcturus Publishing
Distributed by Black Rabbit Books
P.O. Box 3263
Mankato, Minnesota 56002

Printed in China

Planned and produced by Discovery Books Ltd.
www.discoverybooks.net
Managing editor for Discovery Books: Rachel Tisdale
Editors: Amy Bauman and Juliet Mozley
Designer: D. R. ink
Consultant: Xanthe Fry, School Counselor and Educational Consultant
Editor for U.S. edition: Amy Bauman
Picture researcher: Tamsin Osler

Library of Congress Cataloging-in-Publication Data

Kramer, Ann.
  Drugs / Ann Kramer.
      p. cm. -- (Teen FAQ)
  Includes index.
  ISBN 978-1-84837-704-2 (library binding)
  1. Drug abuse--Juvenile literature. 2. Drugs--Juvenile literature. 3. Drugs of abuse--Juvenile literature. I. Title.
  HV5809.5.K73 2011
  613.8--dc22
                          2010010639

Picture credits
Corbis: cover, 9 (Falko Updarp), 20 (Scott Houston/Sygma), 35 (Bob Thomas), 36 (Mediscan), 40 (LWA-Dann Tardif). Getty Images: 13 (Supernova), 14 (Dimas Ardian/Stringer), 17 (Steve Allen), 19 (Chris Jackson), 32 (Luca Zampedri). Istockphoto.com: 7 (Alexandr Tovstenko), 16 (Achim Prill), 26, 27 (Jean-Joseph Renucci), 28 (Henk Bentlage), 31 (Patricia Furtado), 41 (Rich Legg), 45. Photofusion: 10 (Janine Wiedel), 18 (Janine Wiedel), 21 (David Hoffman). Shutterstock: 22 (Gregor Kervina), 24 (Attila Huszti), 38 (Wikus Otto).

Every attempt has been made to clear copyright. Should there be any inadvertent omission, please apply to the publisher for rectification.

SL001458US
Supplier 03, Date 0510

Contents

1 What are drugs?

It seems that barely a day goes by without a newspaper article or a television program about the growing problem of young people using drugs or about a teenager who has died after taking drugs in a club. Sometimes it may feel as if it's one of the most important topics in the media today.

But what do people mean when they talk about drugs? Are they only talking about illegal drugs such as marijuana or heroin? Do they mean other kinds of drugs, too? And how big is the problem?

Defining drugs

Drugs are **chemical** substances that change the way we feel, the way we behave, or how our body works. They can be swallowed, inhaled, or injected. They then enter the bloodstream and affect our bodies and minds in various ways.

Usually when people talk about drugs, they are referring to **street drugs**. These include drugs such as marijuana, cocaine, ecstasy, or heroin, which are illegal in many countries, and which people take for excitement, relaxation or to feel good. Many are harmful, and several are addictive.

Not all drugs that people take are illegal. Alcohol, nicotine (as in cigarettes), and caffeine are drugs. Medicines that doctors prescribe, such as painkillers or tranquilizers, are also drugs. And they can be addictive, too. Then there are solvents and household products such as paint thinners and lighter fuel. These are deadly poisonous, but some people use them as drugs to get high.

When someone says "drugs," what do you think of first? Do you think of medicine, illegal drugs, or something else?

Is there a problem?

Drugs can have devastating effects and may cause **addiction**, lasting physical and mental harm, and even death. There are concerns that teenage **drug misuse** causes problems at school, involves teenagers in criminal acts, and leaves teenagers vulnerable to sexual and other attacks.

NOTHING NEW

Humans have been using drugs for pleasure or as medicine for thousands of years. **Archaeologists** have found evidence that humans were growing marijuana more than 14,000 years ago. The ancient Sumerians used opium more than 5,000 years ago, and Inca peoples chewed coca leaves, the source of cocaine, as part of their religious rituals. Originally most drugs were natural and came from plants; today many are made in laboratories.

Types of drugs

Drugs can be divided into different groups.

- **Stimulants** speed up messages in the brain and along the **central nervous system**, making you feel more alert and energetic and heightening your senses. They include amphetamines, cocaine and **crack**, nicotine, and caffeine.

- **Depressants** slow down the central nervous system. Thinking and activity slow down. Alcohol is a depressant, as are heroin and solvents such as glue and aerosols.

- **Hallucinogens** alter the way you see things, and can cause hallucinations so that you see things that are not there. They include LSD (lysergic acid diethylamide) and "magic mushrooms."

Some drugs don't fit neatly into these groups because they have more than one effect. For instance, marijuana can both stimulate and depress the body, and can cause hallucinations.

Most dangerous

It is hard to say which drugs are most dangerous. Heroin kills more people each year than ecstasy. Drug deaths in the United Kingdom from 1996 to 2005 were 6,913 for heroin compared to 292 for ecstasy. No deaths have been recorded directly and solely from marijuana. But all drugs have unpleasant side effects. If abused, all drugs can be dangerous. Long-term use of any drug can cause permanent damage to the mind and body. And drugs can be difficult to give up.

Teenagers and drugs

In the United States and the United Kingdom, about 9 percent of 11- to 15-year-olds have used an illegal drug. **Drug use** increases with age and it is likely that nearly half of all 17-year-olds will take an illegal drug at least once. Marijuana is the most popular street drug used by teenagers.

Do you know if any of your friends have tried drugs? If so, which ones?

2 Why do people take drugs?

When teenagers are asked why they take drugs, some of the main reasons they give are:

- because they're available
- to have fun and feel good
- to relax and forget problems
- to experiment and be rebellious
- to fit in.

Taking drugs can have a major impact on your life—some users end up homeless.

Not all teenagers who use drugs are addicted to them. But for some teenagers, things can go wrong. They become dependent on drugs, and their lives spiral out of control. Fortunately, most teenagers who use drugs come to no significant harm. They take drugs occasionally, for recreation, in a relatively controlled way, and eventually move on to another way of spending their free time.

Unpredictable effects

Drugs are unpredictable. There is no knowing in advance what a drug will do to you. Each type of drug works differently. Effects vary according to:

- how pure the drug is (meaning whether there are other ingredients in the drug or not—an impure drug will have other, unknown substances mixed with it)
- how a user takes the drug—smoking, inhaling, drinking, or injecting
- the user's age, size, weight, and health
- a user's mood at the time
- where the user takes the drug—for example, alone, with friends, in a club.

There is also the **come down** to think of. This occurs when the effects of a drug wear off, and it happens because your body is working to restore order and clear the toxic substance (the drug) from your system. A come down is usually linked to stimulants such as cocaine or amphetamine and can be so devastating that people take more of the drug in order to avoid the depression, lethargy, and severe low mood that follows a high.

IT HAPPENED TO ME

I started taking drugs when I was about 13. I was bored and didn't have many friends, so it seemed like something to do. At first I just smoked marijuana on the weekend but one day someone offered me some **speed** [an amphetamine]. I was a bit scared, but it made me feel really high and amazing. I took speed every weekend for months. After a while the effects didn't last so long, and someone suggested I try cocaine. Soon I found I needed more and more to get the same high, and it was really expensive. I started stealing money from my mom and took things from the house to sell. I was moody all the time, got into fights, and got expelled from school. I didn't have any money so I started dealing, got busted, and ended up in court. Now my parents want to throw me out.

Tom, 17

I feel left out . . .

Dear Agony Aunt,
Lots of my friends say they have tried drugs. It feels like everyone's taking them, and I'm the only one who isn't. I don't want to miss out on an experience everyone else seems to be having, and I don't want to seem boring. So I'd like to try drugs, but I only want to try milder ones, just so I don't feel left out. Are there any harmless drugs?
Mark, 15

Dear Mark,
Just because some of your friends are using (or say they are using) drugs doesn't mean you have to. Lots of teenagers try drugs because they want to fit in. But that's not a good reason to put your health at risk. Don't let people push you into doing anything you're not comfortable with. You don't have to go along with it just because they want you to—it is your right to say "no." Remember: True friends will like you whether or not you take drugs. And it's not true that everyone takes drugs. At least 50 percent of teenagers never do.

*Most people consider **hard drugs** such as heroin and cocaine to be the most dangerous, and they're very addictive. But every drug, even so-called **soft drugs**, carries its own risks, and you need to be aware of them. Speak to people you trust if you're feeling pressured. Get the facts—look online at web sites such as www.talktofrank.com and make sure you are informed about drugs. You are then in the best position to know your own mind about the whole issue and to make decisions that are best for you. My advice, though, is to stay away from drugs because you don't know where they might lead you.*

Life chances

Regular drug use can damage relationships and life chances. Friends who do not use drugs drift away as a person who uses drugs spends time with other drug users. Because drugs become so important, users spend less time studying and working, and some drop out of school or college, which limits their chances of finding a good job. It can be difficult to cope with teenagers who use drugs.

Some teenagers end up homeless and on the streets, living chaotic and dangerous lives.

Sexual risks

When young people take drugs, they become less inhibited. They may not practice safe sex, such as using **condoms**. They are therefore more at risk of unplanned pregnancies and of sexually transmitted diseases, such as **HIV**. They may also find themselves in unwanted or dangerous sexual situations.

HEALTH WARNING

Drugs may cause:

- problems with weight, as users stop eating proper meals
- a lack of personal hygiene as users stop caring for themselves
- damage to skin and teeth
- damage to the kidneys, liver, and heart
- damage to mental health.

It can be hard to stand out from the crowd by saying "no" to drugs, but always think about what is best for you personally.

Drugs and the law

Drugs aren't just potentially harmful to your mind or body—they are also illegal in most countries. Once you start using drugs, you are breaking the law.

Every year, thousands of people are arrested for drug offenses. Penalties vary according to the drug type and the offense. But it is generally illegal to use, possess, make, or supply drugs to

someone else. A criminal record usually lasts forever and can make it difficult for you to get a job or to travel abroad. If you are underage and police find drugs in your home, your parents will also be in trouble.

Paying for drugs often pushes users into committing crimes to finance their habits. To start with, drugs may seem to be quite cheap. A "tab" (tablet) of ecstasy may cost only as much as a

Getting caught for taking drugs can result in long prison sentences in some foreign countries.

packet of cigarettes. But when people use drugs regularly, or become dependent on them, the cost increases. As people need more money for drugs, they may start stealing or even dealing in drugs.

An illegal trade

Around the world, drugs are an illegal multi-billion dollar industry. Marijuana is homegrown in some cases and then sold to users, although the scale of how much is produced varies and large-scale marijuana "pot farms" are regularly uncovered by the police. Other substances, such as ecstasy, are produced in illegal drug laboratories in places such as Europe and America. The police regularly root out these labs and arrest the individuals involved.

Farms growing drugs such as opium and cocaine are often found in countries such as Afghanistan, Burma (Myanmar), Colombia, and Brazil and then smuggled into the United States, Europe, and elsewhere through a chain of suppliers. These stretch from large **drug cartels**, down through street gangs and middlemen, until they finally end up on the street being sold by individual dealers, who may also be users.

Turf wars can break out between these street dealers or between drug gangs and police. The drug trade as a result is criminal and violent. In the United States, for example, it is estimated that some 5 percent of murders are drug-related.

Criminal organizations that smuggle drugs are often also involved in **people-trafficking,** prostitution, and other criminal activities. This means if you give money to dealers for drugs, you may ultimately be supporting other serious crimes.

"Teens who use drugs are more likely to engage in violent behavior, steal, abuse other drugs, and join gangs."

Office of National Drug Control Policy (ONDC), United States, 2007

LAW ENFORCEMENT

Governments, law enforcement agencies, and customs offices spend huge amounts of money annually trying to interrupt the drugs trade, arresting smugglers, producers, and dealers. One problem is that in some countries, such as Afghanistan, growing drugs provides a living for small farmers. Gangs offer money to poor and young people to entice them into smuggling drugs across borders. In countries such as Thailand, Indonesia, and Singapore, the penalty for drug smuggling may be death. The vast amounts of money involved, the power of major drug cartels, and widespread corruption also make it virtually impossible to end the trade.

3 Marijuana

More teenagers use marijuana than any other street drug. It's the most widely used illegal drug. In the United States, around 30 percent of people aged 15–16 have tried marijuana at least once. In the United Kingdom, the figure is around 20 percent.

What is marijuana?

Marijuana (also called cannabis or dope) comes from a bushy plant, *Cannabis sativa*, which grows wild throughout Asia. Although some is smuggled in from countries such as Morocco and Egypt, it is also "homegrown" in the United States, Canada, the United Kingdom, and elsewhere. The main active chemical is delta-9-tetrahydrocannabinol, or THC. The more THC, the stronger the dose.

Form

Marijuana comes in two main forms: herbal and resin. Herbal, sometimes called weed, is a greenish-brown mixture made from the dried leaves and flowers of the plant. It looks a bit like dried mixed herbs. Resin, often called hash, comes in black or brown blocks and is made by squeezing the sap out of the plant and stem.

Most users mix marijuana with tobacco and smoke it in a hand-rolled cigarette called a "joint" or "spliff." Some smoke it on its own in a pipe called a **bong**. Sometimes people cook marijuana in cookies and cakes and eat it.

Effects

The effects start within a few minutes and may last for several hours. Some teenagers say marijuana makes them feel chilled and relaxed. Users may get giggly and talkative. They are

In 2007, an estimated 6,171 tons (5,600 tonnes) of herbal marijuana and 1,433 tons (1,300 tonnes) of resin were seized worldwide.

HEALTH WARNING

There is no evidence of anyone dying directly from a marijuana **overdose**. However, long-term use can have damaging effects, including:

- tiredness, apathy, and reduced motivation
- poor concentration and difficulty making decisions
- bronchitis and other breathing problems caused by smoking
- risk of lung or throat cancer
- psychological dependence—users think they cannot cope without marijuana
- mental health problems, such as anxiety, paranoia, and even hallucinations or paranoid delusions, particularly if the user already has an underlying problem
- infertility—using marijuana regularly reduces a man's sperm count and can stop ovulation in women. It may harm an unborn child.

more aware of color and music, and time seems to slow until minutes seem like hours. Users often get very hungry. Short-term memory is affected so users may forget what they are talking about. Someone who uses marijuana for the first time may feel sick and panicky. High doses or powerful forms of marijuana, such as **skunk**, can cause hallucinations and feelings of paranoia.

Addiction

Addiction to marijuana depends on factors such as how long you've been using it and how much you use. If you've only been using for a short while, there should be no problem stopping, but with continued, regular use, it can become harder. You may find you have difficulty stopping regular use, and some users experience psychological or physical withdrawal symptoms. Mixing marijuana with tobacco can lead to nicotine addiction as well.

Will I get addicted?

Dear Agony Aunt,
I've smoked marijuana a few times with friends, and I like it. It made me feel good—I was all relaxed and talkative with my friends, when usually I'm very quiet. But I'm worried that there might be bad side effects. I thought marijuana wasn't meant to be as bad as drugs like heroin—after all, you hear about people taking marijuana for medicinal reasons; don't you? But some people say that smoking it leads to harder drugs. I've also heard that it can be addictive. Is that true? Everyone seems to say something different.
Sarah, 15

Dear Sarah,
There are a lot of different opinions about marijuana. Some say it is a "gateway" drug, leading on to other more dangerous drugs. But there's little solid evidence for this. People who use "hard" drugs, such as heroin, probably have used marijuana, but one does not necessarily lead to the other. But because you are using an illegal drug, you are more likely to meet people who will offer you other drugs. Most people say marijuana is not physically addictive in the way heroin is. Still it can be habit forming, and long-term use can have serious side effects. The medical benefits of marijuana are disputed. It's best not to develop the habit.

Once formed, habits can be very hard to break.

Marijuana debates

People have argued that marijuana should be made legal because it is not as dangerous as other drugs. Some people believe that marijuana also has medical benefits: it can ease the difficult side effects of chemotherapy (cancer treatment) and can help with multiple sclerosis (MS) because a compound in the drug is said to be able to prevent muscle tremor and spasticity caused by MS. Others argue that marijuana is dangerous, it can do long-term harm, and every year there are stronger and more harmful forms available (see quote below right).

"Grandma" Putt, who was convicted of possessing marijuana after eating it for medicinal purposes to relieve her multiple sclerosis, took part in the marijuana march in London, England during the annual global cannabis campaign in 2005.

ADDICTION AND WITHDRAWAL

When people say a person is addicted to a drug, they mean the person cannot stop taking it and have become dependent on it. Addiction can be physical or psychological. With physical addiction, when users stop taking the drug, they experience bodily withdrawal symptoms. When people are psychologically addicted, they think that they cannot cope without the drug, although there would be no physical symptoms if they stop taking it. There is information about treatment options for addiction on page 42.

"According to the [U.K.] Home Office, skunk accounts for 70–80 percent of the cannabis sold on the streets of Britain [in 2009], compared with just 15 percent in 2002. Skunk contains three times the levels of THC of regular cannabis, which has levels of only two percent, according to the charity Drugscope. This stronger version of the drug can also bring about psychotic attacks, even in those with no previous psychiatric history."

Guardian, November 6, 2009

FAQ

4 Club drugs

For some teenagers, going out clubbing means taking drugs. The drugs they take are sometimes known as "club" or "dance" drugs because teenagers or young adults take them so they can dance all night. The best known and most widely used is MDMA, known as ecstasy. Others include ketamine and GHB. All have unpleasant side effects, and, in some situations, they can be dangerous.

Ketamine can cause hallucinations in high doses.

Club drugs are often in the news but the percentage of young people who use them is quite small—probably between 1 and 5 percent of 17-year-olds. Users say the drugs make a night out more intense and exciting. But often teenagers may not know what they're taking: they arrive at a club, and someone sells them something saying it will make them feel good.

What is ecstasy?

Ecstasy's chemical name is methylenedioxymethamphetamine, or MDMA for short. It is a stimulant and hallucinogenic. Ecstasy releases mood-altering chemicals in the brain that make the user feel energetic, ecstatic, and full of love.

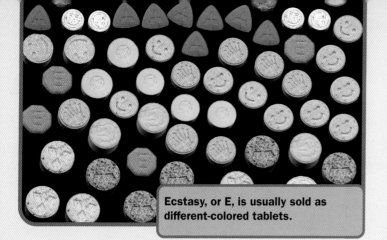

Ecstasy, or E, is usually sold as different-colored tablets.

Effects

Effects start after about 30 minutes and may last for some hours. Users get an energy rush and feel a sense of **euphoria**, music sounds louder, the beat pounds, and they can dance for hours. Users say they feel loving toward the people around them and completely in tune with their surroundings.

Other effects are less pleasant. They include a pounding heart, dry mouth, raised pulse, clenched jaw, and grinding teeth. Users may feel nauseous, paranoid, panicky, and confused. Once the drug wears off, depression sets in and may last for several days—this is part of coming down.

Addiction

Users may develop a **tolerance** to ecstasy, but it is not as physically addictive as drugs such as heroin. There is no physical dependence, no cravings; when quitting, users have only minor effects, such as fatigue, that wear off in a few days. Users may develop a psychological dependence, however, and think they cannot cope without the drug.

Overdose

Excessive doses of ecstasy can result in increased body temperature, tremors, seizures, heart attack, brain hemorrhage, and even death. The United States reported 63 ecstasy-related deaths in 2000.

"Ecstasy gave me the most amazing, thrilling buzz . . . you literally 'feel' the music, and you dance and dance and dance . . . [but] a high is often followed by a low . . . after I have taken ecstasy, I feel very low and depressed . . ."

www.talktofrank.com

"Many smart teens are turning their backs on MDMA."

National Institute on Drug Abuse (NIDA), United States

Will I get addicted?

Dear Agony Aunt,
My friends and I go clubbing every weekend. We usually take E and drink alcohol, too, because then we can dance all night. Until a couple of weekends ago, we were all OK. But then I took some ketamine with alcohol—I was told it would be fun and different—but I collapsed. I don't remember what happened next, but I had to be taken to the hospital by ambulance. I'm better now, but it was the most frightening thing that's ever happened to me. My friends said they thought I was going to die at the time. How come this never happened before?
Paloma, 16

Dear Paloma,
*You were lucky to have survived. There is no way to know whether anyone will collapse if they mix alcohol and drugs like this, as there's always a chance. It is dangerous to mix drugs and alcohol, and especially dangerous to drink alcohol with drugs like GHB and ketamine, or "downers" such as heroin or tranquilizers. Even alone, club drugs have unpleasant side effects. If you add alcohol, it can kill you. Some club drugs may also be linked to what is known as "**date rape**," where drugs are slipped into someone's drink and then they are raped while semiconscious.*

The hot atmosphere of a crowded club can add to the danger of using drugs.

What are ketamine and GHB?

Ketamine, also known as K, is a "dissociative" **anesthetic**. It depresses the central nervous system, causing hallucinations and the "K" hole feeling of being detached from your body.

GHB stands for gammahydroxybutrate. It produces a feeling of euphoria and can reduce your inhibitions. It is also an anesthetic and **sedative**, so it can make you feel sleepy. Initially marketed as a bodybuilding drug, GHB is now illegal. In the United States, it is classed as a Schedule 1 drug, along with heroin and cocaine.

Form

Ketamine, or K, usually comes as a white powder or tablet. GHB, sometimes known as "liquid" ecstasy, is a colorless, tasteless liquid, sold in small bottles.

Effects

Ketamine has caused reported experiences such as hearing sounds that are not there, the feeling of traveling by tunnel into "the light" at high speed with the conviction of having died, and out-of-body experiences. GHB can cause euphoria, lightheadedness, and a feeling of being drunk.

Ketamine and GHB carry serious risks. These include nausea, vomiting, and breathing problems. Ketamine can cause numbness and make movement difficult.

They are both anesthetics, so, if you hurt yourself, you may not know it.

Addiction

Ketamine is not physically addictive, but, psychologically, thanks to its desirable effects and short duration, it can be extremely habit forming. Addiction to GHB can develop in a few weeks and is often characterized by round-the-clock dosing.

Overdose

High doses can lead to unconsciousness, coma, and maybe death. Taking alcohol or ecstasy at the same time as ketamine and GHB may also kill.

STAYING SAFE

- Beware of drugs sold in clubs; many of them are mixed with other substances.
- If you are going to take a drug, tell friends you trust, and stay with them.
- Take regular, small sips of water and rest every so often.
- Never mix drugs with alcohol.
- Never leave a drink unattended.
- Call emergency services immediately if a friend who has taken drugs collapses or complains of feeling very unwell.
- Know as much as possible about any drugs being sold.
- Never accept a drink from someone you do not trust.
- Don't share or exchange drinks.

FAQ

5 Amphetamines and cocaine

Some drugs seem to give users lots of energy and make them very talkative. These types of drugs belong to a group called stimulants and include amphetamines and cocaine. They stimulate the nervous system.

What are amphetamines?

Amphetamines are man-made drugs. Various types are often referred to as speed, because they make users feel more energetic and talk faster.

Form

Amphetamines can be in pill form but are usually sold as a chalky-white or pinkish powder (in wraps), which users sniff, or snort, through the nose. Sometimes users dissolve the powder in liquid (usually water) and inject it. It can also be swallowed. Amphetamines are often mixed or "cut" with all sorts of other substances, such as baking powder or talcum powder, that can be fatal. According to some research, amphetamines tend to be 50 percent pure or more, though this is falling.

Effects

Effects last between three and six hours. Users get a rush of energy. They may feel

Amphetamines speed up messages to and from the brain and can give you a sense of rushing forward.

more alert, excited, confident, and chatty and have a rush of ideas and thoughts.

Unpleasant effects include a racing heart, sweating, headaches, clenched jaw, teeth grinding, loss of appetite, and inability to sleep. As the effects wear off, and users come down, they feel tired, anxious, and depressed.

Addiction

Amphetamines are highly addictive, and short-term recreational use can slip unnoticed into long-term systematic abuse. The body quickly builds tolerance to amphetamines with regular use, though this can fade just as quickly if the user stops taking them. This tolerance means users have to increase doses rapidly to maintain effects. If you are addicted, withdrawal will give exactly the reverse effects of the drug. Instead of the drug's euphoria and curbing the need to eat and sleep, withdrawal causes excessive hunger and fatigue.

Overdose

An amphetamine overdose is rarely fatal but can lead to a number of different symptoms, including **psychosis**, chest pain, and **hypertension**. Amphetamine psychosis usually only occurs with large doses.

Crystal meth

Methylamphetamine or methamphetamine is a type of amphetamine. It is an extremely powerful and addictive stimulant. The crystalline form (commonly referred to as crystal meth) can be easily smoked, and its effects can last between 4 and 12 hours. Crystal meth can bring on a feeling of exhilaration; people feel more awake. It also suppresses appetite.

HEALTH WARNING

Taking amphetamines can cause:

- intense mood swings
- panic and paranoia
- eating and sleep disorders
- heart and blood pressure problems
- tolerance, dependence, and addiction
- overdose
- infections when injecting, particularly if users share needles (see page 35).

IT HAPPENED TO ME

I used to do a lot of speed. To start with, it was great. I seemed to have loads of energy, and I felt as if I could do anything. But I drove my friends mad. I couldn't stop talking, and I couldn't sit still. I couldn't sleep, and I lost loads of weight. When the speed wore off, I was so low and depressed that I just took more. By the end, I was feeling really paranoid. I thought everyone was out to get me. My parents were really worried. Eventually I got help, and now I'm off drugs altogether.

Alvaro, 15

My friend says it's really dangerous . . .

Dear Agony Aunt,
Last weekend I was at a friend's party, and this guy offered me a couple of lines of coke. He said it gives a great buzz and feels really cool. My best friend was sitting beside me on the sofa, and she said it's really dangerous. I said "no" to the guy, because my friend seemed to think it was a really bad idea. But trying it just once can't do me any harm—can it? Isn't my friend just being too cautious?
Isabel, 14

Dear Isabel,
You should listen to your best friend. Coke is dangerous, and many people have died from cocaine overdoses. It's also very addictive. Once hooked, it's hard to get off cocaine; you need more to feel the same effect. If you take coke, your body is put under great pressure—it makes your heart beat faster and can increase your blood pressure and breathing, too. You can suffer from strokes, heart attacks, and seizures. Trying coke even once could kill you. I'd advise you to say "no" if you are offered it again.

A line of cocaine is usually around 50–75 mg.

What is cocaine?

Cocaine, often known as coke or C, is made from the leaves of the coca plant, which is cultivated in various South American countries. Crack is a very powerful form of cocaine.

Form

Cocaine is usually sold as a white powder and is snorted up through the nose. Some users mix cocaine with a liquid (usually water) and inject it. Crack consists of small lumps ("rocks"), and it is smoked. It's called "crack" because of the cracking sound it makes when it is smoked.

Effects

The effects of snorting cocaine start quickly and last for about 30 minutes. Smoking crack produces an almost immediate rush that wears off within about 10 minutes. Users feel on top of the world and very alert, and lose their appetite. As the drug wears off, these sensations are replaced by an intense

Users sometimes snort lines of cocaine with rolled-up dollar bills.

depression. The drug abuser will then "crash," becoming very sleepy. Because the effects wear off quickly, this encourages the user to repeat the experience.

Addiction

Cocaine addiction can occur very quickly and can be very difficult to break. Dependency can develop in less than two weeks. As the person develops a tolerance to cocaine, higher and higher doses are needed to produce the same level of euphoria. The symptoms of cocaine addiction include, for example, heart problems, neglect of responsibilities, social isolation, lack of hygiene, mood swings, and loss of appetite.

Overdose

The symptoms of a cocaine overdose are intense and generally brief. The exact amount of cocaine that causes an overdose depends on factors such as your weight, **metabolism**, or health. A cocaine overdose may cause seizures, heart attack, brain hemorrhage, kidney failure, stroke, convulsions, tremors, delirium and even, in some instances, death.

"From 2002 to 2008, rates of current use among [U.S.] youths aged 12 to 17 declined significantly for illicit drugs overall and for several specific drugs, including marijuana (from 8.2 to 6.7 percent), cocaine (from 0.6 to 0.4 percent), prescription-type drugs used nonmedically (from 4.0 to 2.9 percent) ... and methamphetamine (from 0.3 to 0.1 percent)."

The 2008 National Survey on Drug Use and Health, SAMHSA, U.S. Dept. of Health and Human Services

6 Hallucinogenic drugs

Some drugs distort reality: you see and hear things that seem real but are not actually there. These drugs are called hallucinogens. They include natural substances, such as mescaline and psilocybin that come from plants, and drugs made in laboratories, such as LSD, or **acid**. The most commonly used are "magic mushrooms" and LSD.

What are magic mushrooms?

These are wild mushrooms, or fungi. They are called "magic" because they contain chemicals that alter the senses in quite powerful ways.

In the past, some people used fly agaric mushrooms to kill flies. Small pieces would be added to a saucer of milk and flies that fed on the milk were poisoned by the chemicals.

Young people mainly take liberty cap, a small, pale yellow mushroom on a thin stalk with a pointed cap. Its active ingredient is the hallucinogenic chemical psilocybin. Some people also take fly agaric, a bright red mushroom with white spots.

Form

Hallucinogenic mushrooms are eaten raw or dried, or they may be boiled up in liquid. They taste unpleasant. They can also be smoked.

Effects

It takes about 30 minutes for magic mushrooms to start working and effects can last for four to six hours. Some teenagers say magic mushrooms make them feel happy, giggly, and detached from the world around them. Many hallucinate, seeing or hearing things that are not there. But some people find the experience very scary. A bad **trip** can leave lasting anxiety and paranoia. Users may feel sick and panicky.

Addiction

Mushrooms are not physically addictive. However, as with other drugs, their psychological effects can be very strong, meaning users may think that they cannot cope without the drug.

Overdose

Deaths exclusively from overdose of magic mushrooms are extremely rare. For example, between 1993 and 2000 in the United Kingdom only one death was directly from magic mushrooms compared to 5,737 from heroin. Deaths generally occur due to suicide, accidents, and dangerous behavior brought on by the drug. Others are due to users inadvertently eating poisonous plant material.

HEALTH WARNING

Risks of magic mushrooms can include:

- feelings of anxiety and paranoia
- poisoning (it's easy to pick the wrong type of mushroom)
- accidents caused by lack of coordination, such as when using machinery.

SHAMANIC RITES

Shamans and other religious people have used hallucinogenic plants in spiritual and religious ceremonies for thousands of years. They believed the plants gave them access to the spirit world. Since the 1970s, teenagers and young adults have used hallucinogenic mushrooms for fun and as a more natural alternative to LSD.

"One official survey suggests that between 1998–2004, around 2 percent of 11- to 15-year-olds in England have tried magic mushrooms."

DrugScope

Seven hits, and you're out?

Dear Agony Aunt,
I've heard lots of weird things about acid from my friends, and there are all sorts of stories about it online. Is it true that it can cause brain damage by putting holes in your brain or that it can make you think you are able to fly? I also read that if you take LSD seven times, you go crazy, and that it stays in your system forever. Is any of this true?
Jaime, 14

Dear Jaime,
There are some weird stories about LSD, or acid as it's also called. Some are myths, and some are exaggerated. Once you start a trip, it cannot be stopped, and your experience can vary depending on your mood at the time. Every user's experience is different, so some people may think they can fly. There is no evidence that taking LSD does any long-term damage to the body or mind. However, people have been known to harm themselves if they have a bad trip. It's especially dangerous for people with an existing mental illness.

What is LSD?
LSD stands for lysergic acid diethylamide. It's a hallucinogenic drug that originally came from **ergot**, a fungus found growing wild on rye and other grasses. Today it is made in illegal laboratories. It was developed in 1938 and used in psychiatric treatments. A lot of young people took it during the 1960s, when it was part of the hippie psychedelic culture, and again in the 1980s and 1990s as a club drug.

Form
LSD is usually soaked into small squares of blotting paper or gelatine, which are known as tabs. Sometimes it comes in tiny pills (microdots), which are very strong. Users then swallow it or dissolve it under their tongue. LSD is

powerful. Doses are measured in millionths of a gram (micrograms); a dose of 30 to 40 micrograms is enough to last several hours.

Effects
LSD begins to work within an hour of swallowing a tab and may last for 12 hours. Its effects during this time are known as a trip. Experiences vary enormously. Time and movement seem to speed up or slow down. Colors and sounds appear more intense, and familiar objects take on strange shapes. Sometimes stationary objects seem to move. LSD distorts reality, so someone who takes it may see, hear, or imagine things that are not there. It can also cause **"flashbacks."** These usually involve visual hallucinations, but they

can involve other senses such as taste, smell, and touch. These flashbacks may last a few seconds or minutes.

Other unpleasant side effects include panic and paranoia. It is particularly dangerous for people with a history of mental illness or who are on anti-depressants to take LSD.

Addiction
LSD has no physical addiction potential. However, as with many drugs, users can (and do) become psychologically dependent on LSD, perhaps using it as an escape from reality.

Overdose
There are no deaths known to have resulted directly from an LSD overdose. However, LSD has been related to suicides, accidental deaths, murders, and self-inflicted wounds.

> **"In 2007, more than 22.7 million persons aged 12 or older reported they had used LSD."**
> **National Institute on Drug Abuse**

Experimentation with LSD and other psychedelic drugs, often at concerts or music festivals, was a major feature from the 1960s onward.

FAQ

7 Heroin

Not many teenagers take heroin compared to other drugs, though numbers are increasing. For example, 1.5 percent of eigth, tenth, and twelfth graders reported lifetime use of heroin in a 2005 survey. Heroin is described as one of the "hard" drugs. It's dangerous and powerful, and it can have very serious health risks.

What is heroin?

The medical or scientific name for heroin is diamorphine hydrochloride. It is processed from morphine, which is extracted from the seedpod of the opium poppy. Street heroin comes from poppies grown in Afghanistan, Iran, and Pakistan, and also Burma, Laos, and Colombia. It is a depressant, which means that it slows down the bodily systems.

Smoking heroin gives a quicker but milder effect than injecting or snorting it.

Form

Heroin, also known as H or smack, can be snorted, smoked, or injected.

Effects

When heroin is injected the effects, sometimes known as a "hit," can be almost instant. Users say they feel euphoric. After the initial rush, a person's breathing and heart rate slow right down, as does their thinking. Heroin is an anaesthetic or **opiate**, so mental and physical pain disappear, which is one of the reasons why people take heroin—to get away from their problems. The user may feel warm, drowsy, and detached from life for some hours until the effects wear off.

First-time users often feel sick and may vomit. Tolerance builds up quickly, so users need to take more heroin to get the same effect. Smoking heroin is less dangerous than injecting, but it has risks.

Addiction

Heroin is highly addictive and causes physical dependence, meaning withdrawal symptoms may occur if use is reduced or stopped. Withdrawal produces drug cravings, restlessness, muscle and bone pain, insomnia, and diarrhea and vomiting, among other symptoms. Major withdrawal symptoms peak between 48 and 72 hours after the last dose and fade after about a week.

Overdose

Symptoms of overdose—which may result in death—include shallow breathing, clammy skin, convulsions, and coma.

HEALTH WARNING

Heroin has many dangers, including:

- damaged veins from injecting
- coma and in some cases death
- infections from using and sharing needles (see page 35).

"Teenagers as young as 15 are experimenting with the highly addictive drug heroin . . . [the] charity DrugScope . . . says addicts spend [$12,000] a year on their habit . . ."

BBC News, April 4, 2000

Is my mom taking heroin?

Dear Agony Aunt,
I think my mom's taking heroin, and I'm frightened that she might die. I found a syringe in the bathroom the other day, and she often seems out of it—sometimes she forgets stuff I already told her, and she never used to do that. She used to get really stressed if things went wrong, too, and now she doesn't even seem to care. Is there any way I can know for sure if she's taking heroin? I don't know whether to ask her straight out or not. And what can I do to help her if she is taking it?
Elise, 14

Dear Elise,
I'm sure you are very worried. Thinking that a close family member may be taking drugs is upsetting, and heroin is particularly dangerous. The impact on the family can be devastating. It's not always easy to know if someone is taking heroin. Signs might include slower reactions, poor memory, switching between wakefulness and drowsiness—some of which your mom seems to be showing. It would be best for you to talk to her. If you don't feel you can, try speaking to another close family member who may be able to offer support. The good news is that there is plenty of help and support out there for your mom if she has a drug problem. Contact a professional or a drug helpline for more advice and support [see page 45 for information].

Injecting

Injecting is the most dangerous method of putting drugs into the body, and it carries high risks. When a drug is injected into a vein, it enters the bloodstream and is carried rapidly to the brain. Effects are felt very quickly. Drugs can also be injected into muscles. The main dangers are:

• overdosing

• infections caused by sharing needles (see opposite)

• gangrene and abscesses caused by missing the vein

• damage caused by crushed-up tablets. Tablet particles may build up in the bloodstream, leading to blocked veins, kidney problems, and other complications, such as **thrombosis**.

Users can reduce risks by never sharing needles and by using drug services where needle exchanges are available.

Tolerance of heroin builds so that users have to take more to get the same effects or to avoid very unpleasant withdrawal effects.

SHARING OR REPEAT USE OF NEEDLES

There is a very high risk when people use the same needle to inject a drug into their system. The dangers of sharing dirty needles can lead to blood-related disorders, including hepatitis B and C, and HIV or **AIDS**. In addition, repeated use blunts the needle and eventually jams the syringe.

FAQ

8 Solvents, steroids, and prescription drugs

Apart from illegal street drugs, there are a host of other substances that are classed as drugs. They include solvents, anabolic steroids, prescription drugs, and some medicines that you can buy at any pharmacist. They're easy to get hold of, and some are legal. But all of them can make you sick, and some can kill you, if abused.

What are solvents?

Solvents are everyday products that some people inhale to get high. Solvent abuse is sometimes known as "glue sniffing," but that's not very accurate because there are thousands of household or workplace products that can be used.

Form

Solvents include glues, paints, gases, aerosols, lighter fuel, nail varnish removers, correcting fluids, paint thinners, and many others. They give off fumes or gases that users inhale.

Effects

Users may inhale the solvent directly, from inside a paper or plastic bag, or put it on a rag. It's known as sniffing or huffing. Once the fumes are inside

When solvent users are huffing, they are not breathing enough fresh air and may suffer side effects from lack of oxygen.

the lungs, they are absorbed into the bloodstream and reach the brain quickly. The effects come on fast and last only a minute or so. Teenagers who have used solvents say it makes them feel as if they are drunk on alcohol. They may vomit. Sometimes users lose consciousness briefly. Afterward they may feel tired and drowsy.

While under the influence, users may slur their speech and look dazed. They may behave recklessly, which puts them at risk of accidents. Long-term use may cause damage to the liver, heart, and kidneys.

Every year, young people die or suffer injury from using solvents. Causes include:

- choking on vomit while unconscious

- heart attack

- suffocation if aerosols are squirted directly into the mouth, freezing the airways

- using solvents in a dangerous situation, such as by a busy road.

Addiction
Solvent addiction causes physical dependence. Users may experience withdrawal symptoms when attempting to stop the habit. They may also become psychologically dependent. Those most likely to become addicted are adolescents and younger children.

Overdose
Solvent abuse is potentially very dangerous because it can cause heart failure. Signs of overdose also include symptoms such as coma, convulsions, or breathing difficulties.

IT HAPPENED TO ME

When I was about 13, I saw some of my friends sniffing lighter fuel. They said it was great. I didn't have anything else to do, so I gave it a try, sniffing it out of a balloon. It came on really fast. I couldn't even see. I just had to sit there and then everything blacked out. When I came to, I was covered in blood. I'd fallen over backward and hit my head on the pavement.

Frankie, 14

"Between 70 and 100 young people [die] from solvent sniffing every year [in the United Kingdom]; some of these . . . will be first-time sniffers."

DrugScope

What are prescription drugs?

As the name suggests, prescription drugs are literally drugs that doctors prescribe. They are drugs that have been specifically prescribed for one person who has had a consultation with their doctor. This means that the drugs are safe only for that person to take in the amounts and situations prescribed. Prescription drugs include painkillers such as dihydrocodeine, Vicodin, or Demerol; anti-depressants such as Nembutal or Valium; and stimulants such as Ritalin, which is used to treat attention deficit hyperactivity disorder (ADHD).

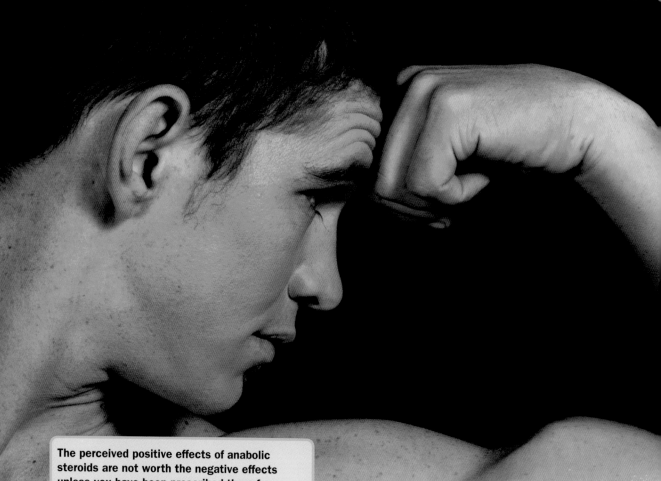

The perceived positive effects of anabolic steroids are not worth the negative effects unless you have been prescribed them for medical reasons.

Recent statistics show that around one in five American teenagers are abusing these drugs. They either steal them from other family members in their own homes or get them from friends.

What are anabolic steroids?

Anabolic steroids, or sports drugs, are often in the news. Anabolic steroids are man-made versions of the male **hormone** testosterone.

Form

Users can inject steroids straight into muscle or take them as tablets.

Effects

Some people believe steroids make them able to train harder in sports, can help build muscle mass and can also help users recover from strenuous exercise faster. For boys, the negative physical effects include lowered **sperm count**, problems with erections, acne, and an increased chance of a heart attack. Girls have problems with periods and may develop facial hair. Both sexes can become very aggressive and violent. Withdrawal symptoms can include headaches, lethargy, and depression.

Addiction

Steroids lead to physical and psychological dependency and addiction. The occurrence of steroid use among high school seniors (4 percent) in the United States was comparable to that for crack cocaine (3.8 percent) or heroin (1.7 percent).

Overdose

The long-term, high-dose effects of steroid use are largely unknown. However, abuse of anabolic steroids may result in serious health damage and death in some cases.

HEALTH WARNING: STEROIDS

Some health risks can be produced by long-term use or excessive doses of anabolic steroids. These effects include harmful changes in cholesterol levels, high blood pressure, liver damage, and dangerous changes in the structure of the left ventricle of the heart.

"As of 2008, teens cite prescription drugs as the second most accessible drugs available to them, after marijuana. Teens also view the drugs as 'safe' highs."

www.streetdrugs.org

"In 2008, 15.4 percent of 12th-graders reported using a prescription drug nonmedically within the past year."

National Institute on Drug Abuse (NIDA), United States

9 Getting help

Every year thousands of teenagers develop problems with drugs. Some end up in the hospital seriously ill; others land in court facing criminal charges. Some die from overdoses; others find themselves increasingly dependent. You may think this cannot happen to you, but it can. It is important to be informed and recognize the danger signs.

Basic safety rules

The only sure way to stay safe is not to use drugs.

- Never be pressured into trying any drug. Make your own decisions; don't let others force you into doing something you do not want to do.

- Buy your own drinks. Never leave a drink where someone can add something to it (spiking it).

Whether you feel at risk of taking drugs or are already doing so, talking to someone can help.

- Stay away from places where drugs are sold and used.

- Stay healthy: eat well and get into active pastimes such as biking, dancing, running, swimming, or going to the gym—these create a natural "high."

However, you may already be taking or thinking of taking drugs.

- Be informed. Find out everything you can about the side effects of drugs, and which ones are addictive.

- Never drive or let anyone else drive if drugs have been taken.

- Be with friends who care about you and your well-being.

- Know what to do in an emergency: Take a first-aid course so that if one of your friends gets ill from drugs, you can give immediate help.

Recognizing danger signs

It is not always easy to know if you or someone else is developing a problem with drugs. Danger signs include:

- relying on drugs to have fun, forget problems, or relax

- panicking if drugs run out

- having blackouts

- taking drugs alone

- withdrawing from friends and family and keeping secrets

- losing interest in school, college, or activities that used to be enjoyable

- performing badly at school or college

- developing a tolerance to drugs

- lying, stealing, or selling things to get money for drugs.

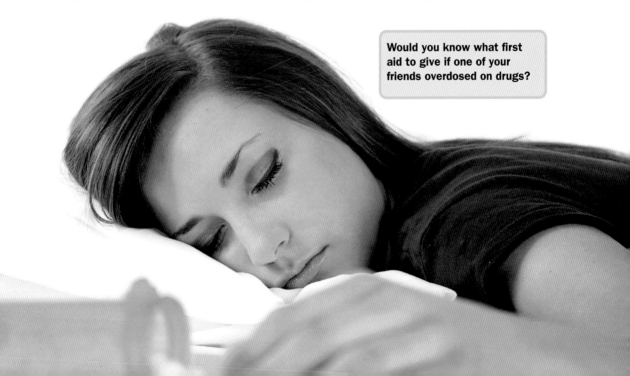

Would you know what first aid to give if one of your friends overdosed on drugs?

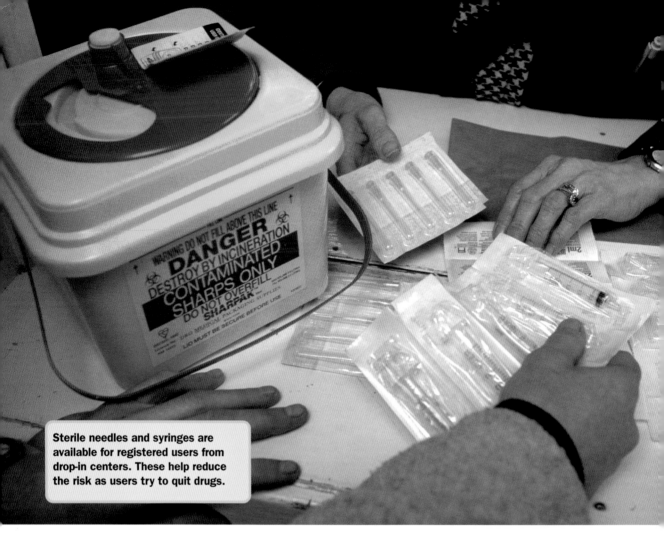

Sterile needles and syringes are available for registered users from drop-in centers. These help reduce the risk as users try to quit drugs.

HEALTH WARNING

Coming off drugs should be done under medical supervision. You can stop using some drugs, such as marijuana, immediately. Others, particularly prescription drugs, have to be cut down gradually. Stopping suddenly can be dangerous. When planning to come off drugs, the best thing to do first is to consult your doctor.

Sources of help

There is a lot of help for young people dealing with drug misuse problems. Help can come from your doctor, a drug counselor or a local drop-in center, drug dependency units, and self-help groups.

Your doctor

Your doctor will ask you questions about your drug habits. Information is confidential—he or she will not talk to your parents or teachers—but it will help the doctor to decide what treatment is right for you. You may need your doctor to refer you to drug treatment programs such as rehabilitation. Rehab programs may include inpatient, residential, and outpatient options in specialist rehab clinics.

Counseling

Counseling or therapy is another option. Having regular sessions with a therapist or drugs counselor will help you understand why you have taken drugs and support you in your efforts to quit—for example, thinking of ways to avoid situations where you might be tempted to take drugs.

Drop-in centers

Street agencies or drop-in centers provide sterile needles and syringes for registered users, counseling, supervised **detoxification,** and other therapies, such as meditation. They can also offer information, advice, and referral to other services.

Units

Residential substance abuse units are usually most appropriate for heavily dependent users who may also have ongoing social and psychological problems. The units specialize in helping drug users—for example, those using drugs such as heroin, cocaine, or prescription drugs—and provide counseling, detoxification, substitute prescribing (the controlled prescribing of medication to users, usually heroin users), and other treatments.

Groups

There are various self-help groups, one of which is Narcotics Anonymous. This is an organization of recovering addicts who attend meetings to help each other stay off drugs. In meetings, members share their experiences with each other in order to reach solutions to their issues. The core of the Narcotics Anonymous program is a series of 12 steps; steps include, for example, admitting to having a drug problem, seeking help, self-appraisal, and supporting other drug addicts who want to recover.

"Almost 24,000 children under 18 received specialist help to tackle substance misuse last year [2008], a 41 percent increase . . . the rise in the numbers of young people in treatment did not mean that more under 18 were misusing drugs . . . rather that access to help was improving."
Guardian, **January 22, 2009**

Glossary

acid street name for LSD (lysergic acid diethylamide) a hallucinogenic drug

addiction dependency on a substance, or behavior, to the extent that it interferes with normal living

AIDS acquired immunodeficiency syndrome. It is a serious disease caused by a virus that destroys the body's natural immune system.

anesthetic a drug that causes a loss of sensation in the body

archaeologists scientists who study the remains of ancient peoples

bong marijuana smoking device that cools the smoke by passing it through water

central nervous system the control center for the body, based in the brain and the spinal cord. It controls all the actions, both voluntary and involuntary, of the body.

chemical a substance with a distinct molecular composition that is produced by or used in a chemical process

come down the after-effect of taking a drug, typically the low that follows a high

condom contraceptive device made of latex rubber that fits over the male penis during sexual intercourse to prevent pregnancy. Condoms also reduce the transmission of sexually transmitted diseases.

crack a very powerful form of cocaine, sold as crystals

date rape a serious sexual assault, usually by a man of a woman, where the attacker is sometimes known to the victim. In some cases, the attacker secretly gives the victim a drug in order to carry out the rape.

depressant something that lowers the heart rate and breathing and suppresses other bodily functions

detoxification a process in which the body is allowed to free itself of a drug

drug cartel criminal organization that controls traffic in illegal drugs

drug misuse when the way a person is using the drug is harmful and a problem. Some people think the term "drug abuse" is too judgmental.

drug use taking drugs

ergot a fungus that infects various cereal plants and forms compact black masses that replace many of the grains of the host plant

euphoria sensations of intense happiness

flashbacks sudden reliving of the experience of taking a drug, particularly LSD, some while after the original experience

hallucinogen a substance that induces hallucinations (false or distorted perception of sights and sounds)

hard drugs used to describe drugs, such as heroin or cocaine, that are seen to be more dangerous than others, that cause dependency and that have higher legal penalties

hepatitis a liver disease. There are various forms. Hepatitis B and C can be caught from injected needles.

HIV human immunodeficiency virus, the virus that can lead to AIDS

hormone a chemical messenger in the body that can affect, for example, growth and development, metabolism, reproduction, and mood

hypertension high blood pressure: a common disorder in which blood pressure remains abnormally high

metabolism the biochemical processes that break down and build up substances from one form to another in the human body, and the energy and exchanges involved

opiate a substance based on opium. It is the base for many drugs, particularly painkillers, and also for cocaine and heroin.

overdose when someone takes too much of a drug. An overdose can be accidental and may be fatal.

people-trafficking the trade in which people are taken away from their home or country and then made to work for no or low payment or with their rights not respected

psychosis any severe mental disorder in which contact with reality is lost or highly distorted

sedative a drug that reduces excitability and calms a person

skunk powerful type of marijuana that has been specially cultivated

soft drugs drugs that are believed to be nonaddictive and less damaging to the health than hard drugs

speed street name for amphetamines, which stimulate the central nervous system, increasing energy and wakefulness

sperm count the number of sperm in an ejaculation; this is used as an indicator of male fertility

stimulant a drug that stimulates or speeds up the central nervous system

street drugs illegal drugs taken for nonmedicinal reasons (usually for mind-altering effects)

thrombosis the formation or presence of a thrombus (a clot of blood) in a blood vessel

tolerance the amount of a drug that someone needs to get the desired effect. The higher someone's tolerance, the more they will need to take to get the same effects.

trip term used to describe the experience of taking a hallucinogenic drug such as LSD or magic mushrooms

turf wars disputes between criminals or gangs over the right to operate within a particular area

Further information

WEB SITES

www.drugfreeworld.org
Foundation for a drug-free world. This web site contains information about drugs and real-life stories.

http://kidshealth.org/teen/drug_alcohol
This web site is part of the series of web sites—for kids, teens, parents—run by the nonprofit Nemours Center for Children's Health Media. One of the sites' goals is to give visitors up-to-date information on health issues, including drug and alcohol use and abuse.

www.streetdrugs.org
A web site for students, teachers, and parents that includes basic knowledge about individual drugs as well as up-to-date news.

www.talktofrank.com
This down-to-earth web site includes an A–Z of drugs and individual stories about using drugs and help getting off drugs.

www.teens.drugabuse.gov
This web site was created by the National Institute on Drug Abuse (NIDA) to give teens, 11 through 15 (as well as their teachers and parents) the information, advice, and real-life stories they need about drug abuse.

HOT LINE

SAMHSA (Substance Abuse and Mental Health Services Administration, U.S. Department of Health and Human Services): Contact 800-662-HELP or http://findtreatment.samhsa.gov to get information about programs and treatment facilities around the United States to deal with alcoholism, alcohol abuse, and drug abuse problems.

BOOKS

K. A. Francis, *Drugs*, (from the Health at Risk series), Cherry Lake Publishers, 2009

Kyle Keegan, *Chasing the High*, Oxford University Press, 2008

Tara Koellhoffer, *Ecstasy and Other Club Drugs*, Facts on File, Inc., 2008

Antony Lishak, *What's That Got to Do with Me?: Drugs*, Black Rabbit Books, 2007

Sarah Medina, *Know the Facts: Drugs*, Rosen Publishing Group, 2009

Index